Miniatures

Carsten René Nielsen & Mette Norrie

Translated by David Keplinger

Plamen
Press
When Words Ignite

Washington, DC

Plamen Press
9039 Sligo Creek Pkwy, suite 1114,
Silver Spring, Maryland 20901
http://plamenpress.org

Translation copyright © 2025 by David Keplinger
Danish text copyright © 2025 by Carsten René Nielsen
Illustation copyright © 2025 by Mette Norrie
Published in Danish by Ekbátana, Copenhagen, 2021
Published by Plamen Press, 2025

Printed in the United States of America

10 9 8 7 6 5 4 3 2 1

Publisher's cataloging-in-publication data
Names: Nielsen, Carsten René, author. Keplinger, David,
translator. Norrie, Mette, illustrator
Title: Miniatures

LCCN: 2025943897
Identifiers: ISBN 978-0-9960722-9-8 (paperback)
ISBN 978-1-951508-47-0 (hardback) | ISBN 978-1-951508-48-7 (epub)
ISBN 978-1-951508-49-4 (pdf)

Subjects:
LCSH: Danish literature—Translations into English.
Danish literature--21th century. | European literature.
BISAC: Poetry/ European / General
Poetry Denmark

Edited by Rachel Miranda
Author's Photograph by Preben Stentoft
Cover Design by Roman Kostovski

Miniatures

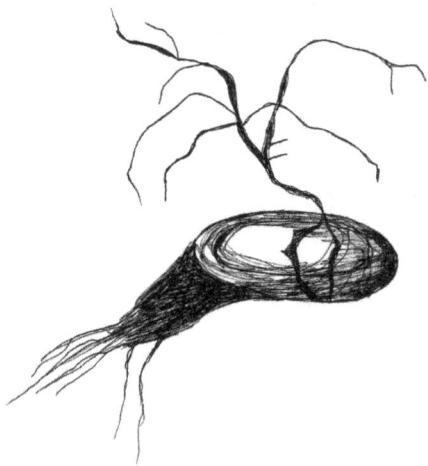

It was a tree

that began

to grow

from a crack

in the old, chipped

plate.

At the security check
a handbag is X-rayed,
and inside the handbag
you can see a handbag
and inside this handbag
yet another handbag
that contains a handbag
with a handbag
that is empty.

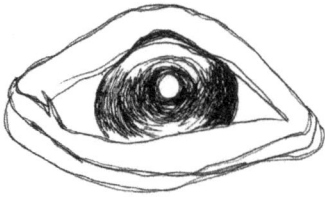

A woman
tenderly rocks
an eye in her arms.

The pond is layered with biscuits.
We have to tread very carefully
to reach the opposite bank.
There are seventy meters of cream
beneath us, and the biscuits crack
with each step.

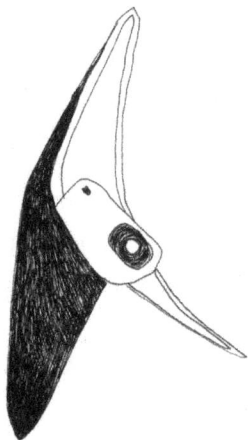

No one is capable
of photographing themselves
when laughing,
for in the laughing
one is no one.

All of us long for a year

when the only news

is that the trees have written themselves

into history, and the snow

has been assigned its own ministry.

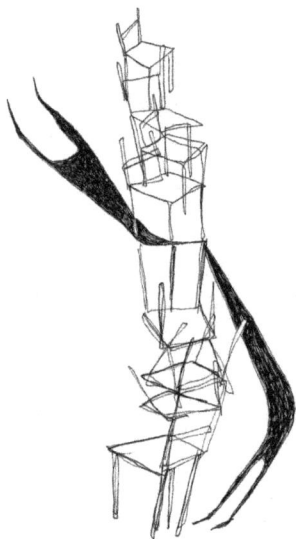

After a long journey
a man comes home
to an identical copy of the building
he lived in before his departure.
Even the furnishings in the apartment
look indistinguishable from those
he once had.

Everything in nature
envies the nature
of beauty.

When our brains become redundant

and can only be seen in museums,

the algorithms will think

that they once were used

in the living lighthouses,

on the sighing steamers,

in the lonely locomotives.

At the library
everyone sits deeply concentrated,
each of them reading their own
hand mirror.

Pieces of your soul
are now for sale
in small gift boxes
at the checkout
in the supermarket.

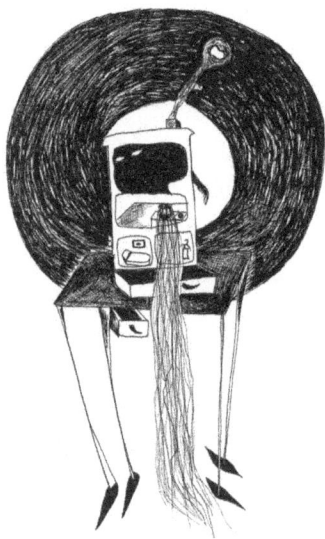

Walking around in a dollhouse
with Joseph Cornell. In the living room
the oversized cat has tipped over,
in the kitchen the hair in the pot is boiling.
As always, coincidence is best
when you play no part in it yourself,
but Cornell is already at work
rummaging through a drawer for things
that coincidentally belong together.

The meaningless
always makes
good sense.

You were a skater
on an ice cream cake,
I a diver inside the vial
of a spirit level.

Between the pages of an herbarium

we found a shrivelled ear

with a few words still inside it.

During the night

the mannequins

have lost a bit of air.

Their cheeks are tired now

like tired cheeks actually are.

The breasts fall

as breasts do.

She is full of stars:
they shine faintly through her skin,
through the thin fabric of her dress.
One of the arms is five meters long,
the other just ten centimeters.
She waves hello with the long arm
and bids goodbye with the short.

Despairingly we walk

back and forth

in the white desert

on the floor of the bathtub.

Our little friends,

the poets,

are being herded together

in an enclosure

behind

the novel factory.

Insects on croquis drawings
can rarely be distinguished from each other,
but occasionally you can see
an ear on a butterfly's wing,
a navel in a beetle's carapace,
a wasp with a nightcap, a cockroach
with eyes in the back of its head.

Shut up already.

Whenever you open your mouth

I hear an orchestra.

Loneliness

is best enjoyed

alone.

Danish noses

very soon now

will all be translated

into English,

and that will be the end

of smelling

in Danish.

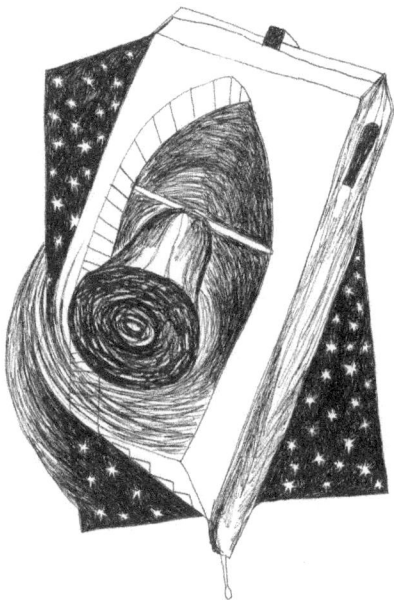

Dark moon:
a black bell
that absorbs all sound
when it rings.

The smallest things
are not so important.
The biggest ones
aren't either.

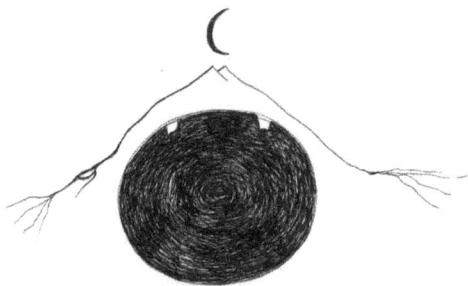

A molar with closed eyes
and an almost innocent nail.
The snoring of your breasts
and your smiling clitoris.
I saw hair in flight in the sky
as I crossed the bridge of the tongue.

After having fried my bacon,
in the middle of the frying pan
I see a man in fat up to his knees
who plays the double bass with his fingers,
very slowly, almost sleepily.
Every time he plucks a string
the sound builds up around the double bass
as rings in the fat, as if time
were played back at half-speed.

The straight and narrow isn't best,

but it is best

for you to stand

sufficiently slanted,

so the houses become

all dizzy.

The animals of humans:
a bleating sheep
in a butter crock,
a bull running around
under a cheese dome.

Before you get into bed
to go to sleep,
you must remember
to turn back
your heart.

My word is my bond,
a star only
a flowering sun.

A painter who insisted
that his colors on the white canvas
were more real than other colors
on white canvases was chased out
of the last surrealist village
by the angry inhabitants
with their soft pitchforks.

The forest has become so pretty
and clean and tidy,
that hand soap now hangs
like fruit on the trees.

"There is not lufficient sight,"
you say, dazed
and unhappy.
"Then try to find
the dight in the larkness,"
I say.

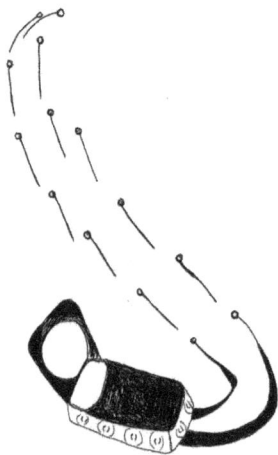

After a long day of hiking

over the pincushion,

it is good to sleep

in the powderpuff case.

A woman sits alone
on a bench in a park.
The birds think
she is Ingrid Bergman
and start chirping
so beautifully in Swedish,
but she does not hear them,
because she doesn't speak
a word of Swedish.

An artichoke with a walking stick,

an egg in a suit,

two steaks both in love

with a heartless beetroot.

Sometimes
the autumn leaves
pretend to be
yellow and brown
butterflies.

Once, umbrellas
rhymed with sleep and cellar.
Now we wash and dry the words
so those who are awake
don't get sad.

After humans:
mountains of cans,
rivers of lost shoes,
oceans only sailed upon
by yellow plastic ducks.

Of course, there is a word
in French for smoothing out
dog-ears: décorner.
In Danish, the books
stand naked on the shelf
and freeze, for lack of
better words.

A man stops you on the street
and lifts up his shirt.
"Look at my navel," he insists.
Hesitantly you bend down and look.
The navel is your mother's mouth.
"When will you get home?"
she says accusingly.

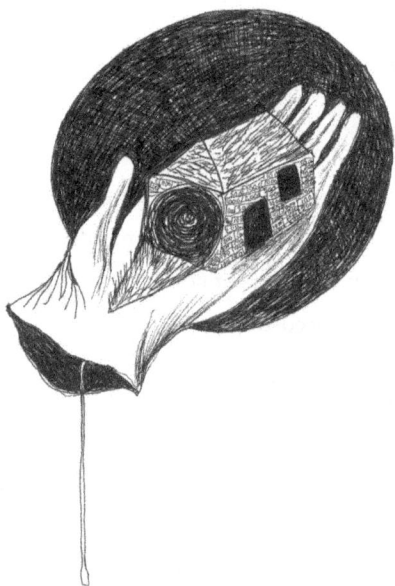

Everything of worth

is worthless.

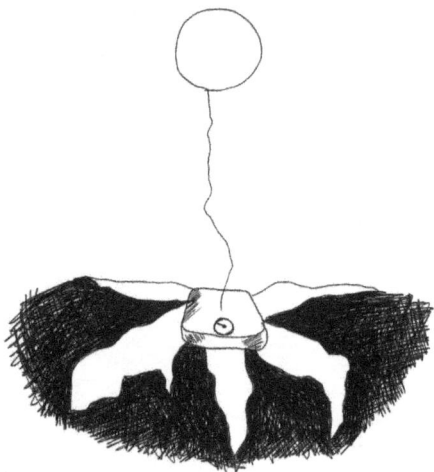

As the continents shift
and the distance to the moon
continues to increase,
I stand completely still
on the bathroom scale
and watch how, very slowly,
I weigh less and less.

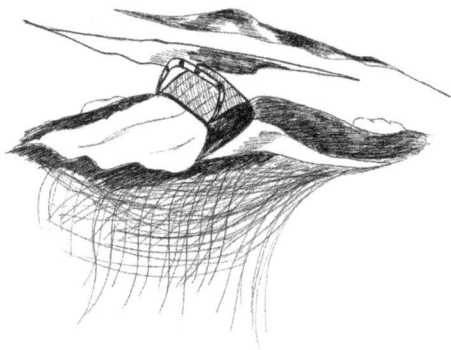

A spider web
in morning sun.
Fields saturated
with silence.
A picnic basket filled
with fog.

About the Author

Danish poet **Carsten René Nielsen** is the author of several poetry collections, including two books of children's poetry. His works in English include the prose poems *The World Cut Out with Crooked Scissors* (New Issues, 2007), *House Inspections* (BOA Editions, 2011), and *Forty-One Objects* (Bitter Oleander Press, 2019), all translated by the American poet David Keplinger. In the United States, his poems have appeared in various journals, including *The Paris Review*, *Circumference*, *Agni*, *Two Lines*, and *Copper Nickel*. He is a recipient of the prestigious Michael Stunge Poetry Prize and The Danish Ministry of Culture's Children's Book Award. His poetry has also has also been published in other countries such as Germany, India, the Netherlands, Italy and Canada. He lives on the island of Samsø in Denmark.

About the Illustrator

Danish artist and author **Mette Norrie** has an MFA from the renowned Royal Danish Academy of Fine Arts in Copenhagen. Her work includes numerous illustrations for both Nordic and international publications, as well as collections of visual poetry, prose, and graphic novels written in Danish and English.

About the Translator

American poet and literary translator **David Keplinger** is the author of eight books of poetry, including *Ice* (Milkweed Editions, 2023), *The World to Come* (Conduit Books, 2021), and *Another City* (Milkweed Editions, 2018), which won the 2019 Rilke Prize. He is the translator of several books of poetry from Danish and German. His translation of Carsten René Nielsen's collection of poems, *Forty-One Objects* was a finalist for the 2020 National Translation Award. He is the recipient of the 2025 Joseph Brodsky Rome Prize from the American Academy in Rome.

www.ingramcontent.com/pod-product-compliance
Lightning Source LLC
Chambersburg PA
CBHW021153090426
42740CB00008B/1065

* 9 7 8 0 9 9 6 0 7 2 2 9 8 *